Adventure Cookery

JUNGLE
EXPEDITION

WRITTEN BY
WENDY-ANN ENSOR

ILLUSTRATED BY
WENDY LEWIS

Evans

Evans Brothers Limited

NOTES TO PARENTS AND TEACHERS

The Adventure Cookery series is intended for use at home or at school. All the recipes have been carefully tested both by my own children and in our classroom kitchen.

Each book begins by introducing the theme and setting of the adventure. There are five recipes in each book linked to the adventure theme and which involve weighing and measuring (both metric and imperial measurements are given). The diagrams and simple step-by-step instructions can be followed by a child, although an adult should always help when the oven is to be used or the cooking involves a gas burner or hotplate.

I have found that if an idea catches a child's imagination an associated activity, such as cooking, can operate as a bridge leading to creative writing, art and craft and the practical application of maths and science. These books will, I hope, help you to provide that bridge.

Wendy-Ann Ensor

Before starting to cook

Remember:

1 Wash your hands and make sure your hair is tied back from your face.

2 Put on an apron.

3 Collect everything you need on the table in front of you.

4 Weigh the exact quantities written in the recipe.

5 If you taste the mixture wash your spoon at once.

6 If you spill anything on the floor wipe it up immediately.

Take care

handles

hot dishes

sharp knives

cooker hotplates

About Jungles

There are big trees, tall grasses and many bushes in the jungle.

In the tangled undergrowth live dangerous animals such as tigers, leopards and wild boar.

Long poisonous snakes slither and slide and monkeys jump from tree to tree.

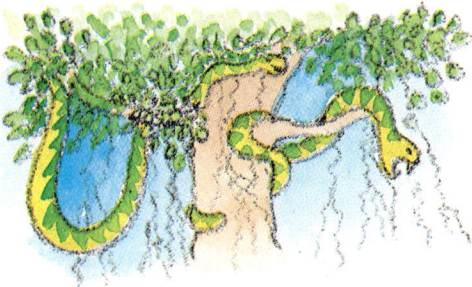

Crocodiles glide through the muddy rivers and colourful parrots sing their songs.

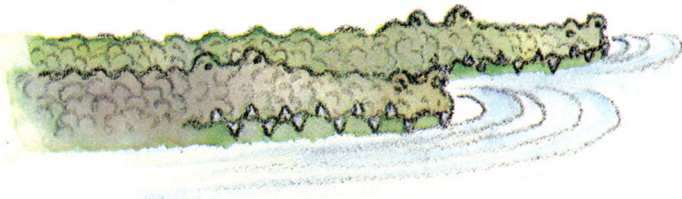

HUNTERS' SANDWICHES

If you have been out hunting all day in the jungle you will be very hungry! Perhaps you had better make some Hunters' Sandwiches.

What to do:

1 Spread the butter or margarine on the slices of bread.

2 Peel the hard-boiled egg and mash it in a basin. Season with salt and pepper.

3 Cut the cress and wash it well.

4 Put a spoonful of egg on a slice of bread and add some cress.

5 Place a buttered slice on top and cut in half corner to corner. Use the egg and cress for as many sandwiches as you can make.

Remember to wrap your prepared sandwiches in greaseproof paper or foil until you are ready to eat them.

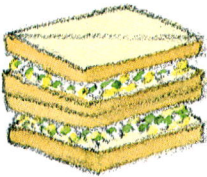

You can buy cress but it is much more fun to grow your own.

What to do:

1 Cover the bottom of your saucer with cotton wool.

2 Wet the cotton wool and shake the cress seeds over it.

3 Put the saucer in a warm, dark cupboard and water it each day.

4 When the cress begins to grow, bring it into the light until it is ready to cut. It will take about a week.

You will need:

1 packet cress
A large saucer
A little cotton wool

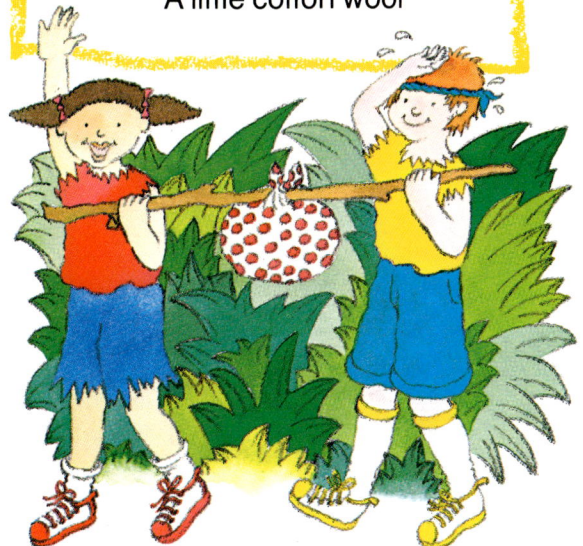

CAMPFIRE SPECIAL

If you are cooking on your Jungle Expedition you will need a campfire. These can be fun but also very dangerous. If you are having a party without an adult you could make a campfire out of cheese pastry sticks and build them round a tomato for the flames.

You will need:

175g (6oz) plain flour
50g (2oz) grated cheese
Salt and pepper
50g (2oz) margarine
1 egg
1 tomato

What to do:

1 Rub the margarine into the flour, add cheese, salt and pepper.

2 Mix with enough egg to make the dough easy to roll.

3 Roll out the dough to about 1cm (½in.) thick and cut into sticks.

4 Bake on a well-greased baking sheet in a hot oven (Reg. 6/ 200°C/400°F) for about 10 minutes.

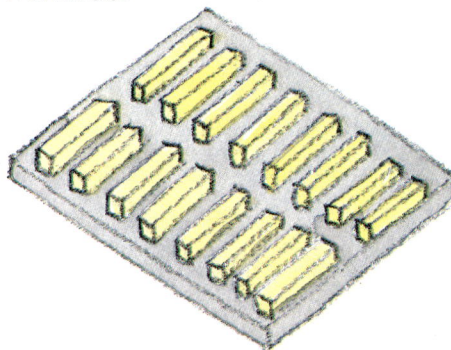

5 When cold arrange over a cut tomato to look like a campfire.

Now your fire is ready to sit around.

MONKEY MUNCHIES

Monkeys are very lively animals. In the jungle they take spectacular leaps from tree to tree and will then sit chattering to each other and munching their food. You could make some Monkey Munchies.

You will need:

150g (5oz) soft margarine
100g (4oz) brown sugar
100g (4oz) unsalted peanuts
150g (5oz) self-raising flour
Paper cake cases

What to do:

1 Put all the ingredients in a bowl and mix well.

2 Put a spoonful of the mixture in each paper case.

3 Cook in a hot oven (Reg. 6/ 200°C/400°F) for about 10 minutes.
Take care the monkeys don't eat all your munchies.

CROCODILE CAKE

Crocodiles are reptiles with a very tough skin which looks like armour. They have their eyes, ears and nostrils at the top of their heads and they have **very** sharp teeth! You wouldn't want to meet a real one on your Jungle Expedition but you could make a Crocodile Cake.

You will need:

1 Swiss roll
1 chocolate flake bar
100g (4oz) icing sugar
A little water
A few blanched almonds
Green colouring
2 cherries

What to do:

1 Cut a small slice out of the Swiss roll to make the mouth. Use this piece for the tail.

2 Put the icing sugar in a basin and add a few drops of green colouring.

3 Add the water, a little drop at a time from a teaspoon, until the icing is soft.

4 Cover your crocodile with green icing and make fork marks for his skin.

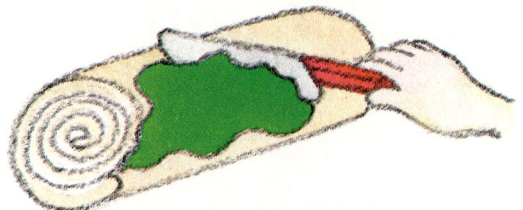

5 Fix the nuts in his mouth for teeth and the two cherries for eyes.

6 Break the flake bar in 4 pieces and use for legs. When you break the bar you will have a few flakes on the board which you can use to put over his back.

This crocodile is very friendly!

JUNGLE JUICE

There are many dangerous animals in the undergrowth like leopards and tigers. Beware the poisonous snakes! You will need to drink some Jungle Juice to make you strong.

You will need:

1 small packet orange juice
1 small packet pineapple juice
1 small can pineapple chunks
A few glacé cherries

What to do:

1 Put the pineapple chunks, cherries, orange juice and pineapple juice in a bowl.

2 Mix well.

3 Put in a jug and keep cool until you are ready to use.

Activity Page

The undergrowth is so thick in your jungle that you will need to make a raft and glide down the river. Watch out for crocodiles in the water and snakes on the bank. The parrots might like some crumbs from your sandwiches and you can hear the friendly monkeys chattering in the trees.

Now you can take some friends on your raft for your Jungle Expedition. When they have enjoyed the food they might like to make some jungle animals with old socks, egg boxes and card.

You will need:

Raft

Box or piece of card.

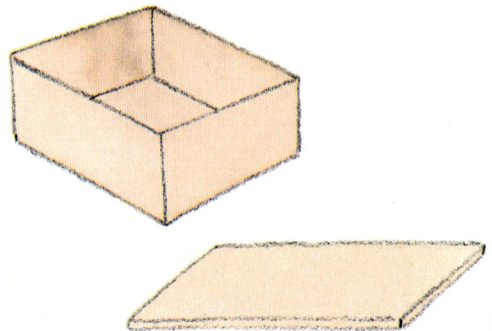

Snake

Woollen sock stuffed with newspaper. Scraps of material for eyes and tongue.

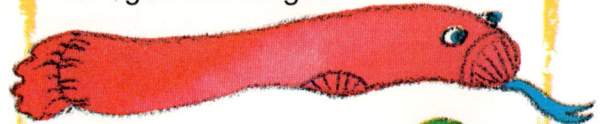

Parrot

Card   Felt tip pens
Scissors   Stick

Crocodile

Egg boxes
Paint